P9-CMR-195

THE
Mauna Loa®
MACADAMIA COOKBOOK

 Leslie Mansfield

CELESTIALARTS

Berkeley, California

Copyright ©1998 by Leslie Mansfield. All rights reserved.
No part of this book may be reproduced or transmitted
in any form or by any means, electronic or mechanical,
including photocopying, recording, or by any information
storage or retrieval system, except for brief review, with-
out the express permission of the publisher. For more
information, you may write to:

CELESTIAL ARTS

P.O. Box 7123
Berkeley, CA 94707
e-mail:order@tenspeed.com
website:www.tenspeed.com

Celestial Arts books are distributed in Canada by Ten
Speed Canada, in the United Kingdom and Europe by
Airlift Books, in South Africa by Real Books, in Australia
by Simon & Schuster Australia, in New Zealand by Tan-
dem Press, and in Southeast Asia by Berkeley Books.

Text design by Greene Design

Printed in Singapore

0-89087-879-X

Library of Congress Catalog Card Number:
98-072530

1 2 3 4 5 6 7 8 9 10 / 08 07 06 05 04 03 02 01 99 98

To Richard,
My husband and best friend,
thank you for a life filled with
adventure shared.

✆ *Introduction*

Mention macadamias and visions of choco-late-glazed clusters of crunchy, buttery heaven come to mind. Although this tropical treat has become synonymous with Hawaii, it is also a versatile ingredient in both sweets and savories. Macadamias enjoy a greater availability than ever before and are being eagerly embraced by chefs around the world, who are delighted by their contribution of creamy flavor and smooth texture. *The Mauna Loa Macadamia Cookbook* celebrates this ver-satility with dishes that are both foreign and familiar, traditional and exotic.

Introduced from eastern Australia in the late nineteenth century, the commercial cultiva-tion of the macadamia tree began in earnest in the 1950s when methods for cracking and removing the hard shell from the nutmeat were developed and perfected. Today, the finest macadamia orchards in the world climb the majestic slopes of Mauna Loa on the Big Island of Hawaii where the volcanic soil, abundant rainfall, and equatorial sunshine provide ideal growing conditions.

Growing macadamias is a time and labor intensive operation. The trees begin to bear nuts at five years old, and don't reach their full bearing potential until fifteen years of age. The trees blossom periodically and yield nuts in waves, requiring five or six harvests annually. Mechanical harvesters collect roughly half the fallen nuts, but crews of hand-pickers are needed to harvest those in less accessible locations. With close to one million trees on ten thousand acres and decades of refining its orchards, Mauna Loa has earned its reputation as the leader in the macadamia nut industry.

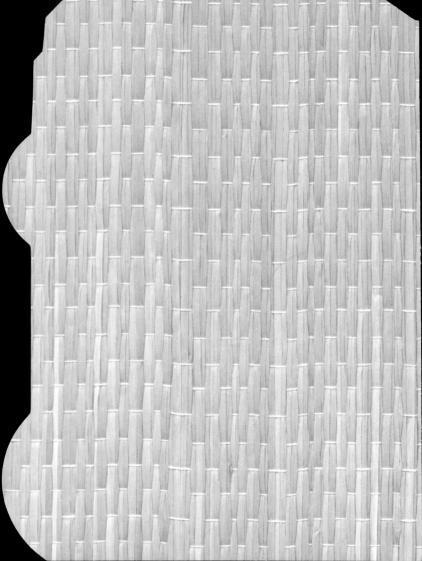

✎ Savories

Onion and Garlic Macadamias

These are wonderful to snack on, or sprinkle on salads for an unexpected touch.

2 tablespoons butter
2 teaspoons minced dried onions
2 teaspoons dry parsley
2 teaspoons salt
1 teaspoon freshly squeezed lemon juice
1 teaspoon onion powder
1 teaspoon sugar
1/2 teaspoon garlic powder
2 cups Mauna Loa macadamias

In a skillet, melt butter over medium heat. Whisk in dried onions, parsley, salt, lemon juice, onion powder, sugar, and garlic powder until smooth. Stir in macadamias. Sauté about 5 minutes.

MAKES ABOUT 2 CUPS

Sweet and Spicy Pepper Nuts

❧ *This is a sophisticated nibble to serve with drinks.*

1/4 cup butter
1/2 cup packed brown sugar
1 tablespoon water
2 teaspoons freshly ground black pepper
1 1/2 teaspoons salt
2 cups Mauna Loa macadamias

❧ Preheat oven to 350 degrees F. Lightly oil a baking sheet.

In a large non-stick skillet, melt the butter over medium heat. Add the brown sugar, water, pepper, and salt and stir to dissolve the sugar. Add the macadamias and cook, stirring often, until syrup thickens and turns a deep brown. Spread onto baking sheet and bake for about 10 minutes. Place baking sheet on a rack to cool. Break into small pieces when cool enough to handle. Cool completely and store in an airtight container up to 2 weeks.

MAKES ABOUT 2 CUPS

Cinnamon-Sugar Spiced Macadamias

✒ *These are delicious during the holiday season.*

1/2 cup sugar
1 1/4 teaspoons cinnamon
1/4 teaspoon ground ginger
1/4 teaspoon salt
1 egg white
2 cups Mauna Loa macadamias

✒ Preheat oven to 300 degrees F. Lightly oil a baking sheet.

Stir the sugar, cinnamon, ginger, and salt together with a fork until blended. Whisk in the egg white until foamy. Stir in the macadamias. Spread mixture onto the prepared baking sheet and bake for 10 minutes, stir, and bake an additional 10 minutes. Cool and store in an airtight container.

MAKES ABOUT 2 CUPS

Fruit Salad with Macadamias

✦ Serve this cool and refreshing salad during the dog days of summer.

Dressing:

1/4 cup sugar
2 tablespoons orange liqueur
1 tablespoon freshly squeezed lime juice
1 tablespoon minced fresh mint

2 cups cubed cantaloupe
2 cups cubed mango
2 cups cubed pineapple
2 cups halved strawberries
1/2 cup finely chopped Mauna Loa
  macadamias

✦ For the dressing: In a small bowl, whisk together sugar, orange liqueur, and lime juice until sugar dissolves. Whisk in mint.

In a large bowl, combine cantaloupe, mango, pineapple, and strawberries. Pour dressing over and toss well. Sprinkle with macadamias and serve.

SERVES 8

Macadamia-Crusted Monterey Jack

1 baguette, cut into 1/2-inch thick slices
1 large clove garlic, cut in half
1/2 cup all-purpose flour
1 egg, lightly beaten
1 cup finely chopped Mauna Loa macadamias
12 ounces Monterey Jack cheese, cut into
   about eight 1/2-inch thick slices
3 tablespoons Mauna Loa Macadamia Oil

Preheat oven to 350 degrees F.

Place baguette slices in a single layer on a baking sheet. Bake for about 15 minutes, or until lightly toasted. Remove from oven and rub the cut side of the garlic on top of the toasts. Discard garlic.

Place flour in a shallow bowl. Place egg in another shallow bowl. Place macadamias in another shallow bowl. Dredge cheese slices in flour, then dip in egg. Finally, place in macadamias, pressing to coat both sides.

In a large non-stick skillet, heat the oil over medium heat. Add the crusted cheese slices and fry about 5 minutes per side, or until nicely browned on both sides. Place 2 pieces of toast each on 8 salad plates and top with a slice of hot cheese. Serve immediately.

SERVES 8

Around the world,
the macadamia is known
by a variety of names.
In its native Australia,
the aboriginal name is the
Kindal-Kindal.
Other names include the
Queensland nut,
Bauple nut,
and the popple nut.

Brie and Macadamia-Stuffed Mushrooms

✐ Prepare these sensational hors d' oeuvres early and broil at serving time.

1 pound large mushrooms, cleaned
1 tablespoon freshly squeezed
   lemon juice
1 tablespoon butter
1 tablespoon sour cream
1/4 cup finely chopped Mauna Loa
   macadamias
3/4 teaspoon salt
1/2 teaspoon freshly ground pepper
1/4 teaspoon fines herbes
4 ounces Brie cheese

✐ Pull stems out of mushrooms and place mushroom caps on a broiling pan. Finely chop stems and toss with lemon juice. In a sauté pan, melt butter over medium heat. Add chopped stems and sauté until liquid evaporates. Stir in sour cream and sauté until mixture appears almost dry. Transfer mushroom mixture to a bowl. Stir in macadamias, salt, pepper, and fines herbes. Let cool.

Trim the rind off of the Brie and discard the rind. Finely dice the Brie and stir into the mushroom mixture.

Preheat the broiler.

With a small spoon, fill the mushroom caps with the stuffing. Broil until bubbly and golden brown.

SERVES 6

There are two species of macadamias that produce edible nuts. One is the rough-shell macadamia, M. tetraphylla. The other, commonly known as the smooth-shell, goes by the botanical name M. integrifolia.

Although both are grown commercially, most plantings are of the smooth-shell macadamia.

Cream of Tomato Soup with Onion and Garlic Macadamias

Prepare this soup when your garden is overflowing with tomatoes.

3 tablespoons butter
1 onion, finely chopped
3 pounds ripe tomatoes; peeled, seeded and chopped
2 tablespoons packed brown sugar
1 tablespoon minced fresh basil
1 bay leaf
1 teaspoon salt
$1/2$ teaspoon freshly ground black pepper
2 whole cloves
$1\,1/2$ cups half-and-half
1 cup Onion and Garlic Macadamias, see page 2

*In a large stockpot, melt butter over medium heat. Add onion and sauté until very tender. Add tomatoes, brown sugar, basil, bay leaf, salt, black pepper, and cloves and stir well. Reduce heat to low, cover and simmer until tomatoes are cooked through, about 30 minutes. Remove bay leaf and cloves and discard. Purée soup in batches in a blender. Return puréed soup to pot and stir in half-and-half. Heat through over low heat, do not allow to boil. Serve topped with a sprinkle of Onion and Garlic Macadamias.

SERVES 6

> Each macadamia nut tree
> can produce about 100
> pounds of in-shell
> macadamia nuts per year.
> After shelling, only about
> 20 pounds of creamy white
> kernels remain.

Spaghetti with Gorgonzola and Macadamias

ꗥ *Serve with a green salad for a light supper.*

2 tablespoons butter
2 cloves garlic, crushed
4 ounces Gorgonzola, crumbled
1/4 cup sour cream
3/4 cup finely chopped Mauna Loa
    macadamias
Salt and freshly ground white pepper
12 ounces spaghetti

ꗥ In a large saucepan, melt butter over medium heat. Add garlic and sauté until fragrant. Add the crumbled Gorgonzola and stir until melted. Add sour cream and stir to make a creamy sauce. Stir in the macadamias. Season with salt and pepper to taste.

Cook the spaghetti in boiling salted water until *al dente*. Drain the spaghetti thoroughly, then add to the sauce in the pan. Stir gently until coated and serve immediately.

SERVES 4

Spicy Macadamia Noodles

³/4 cup chopped Mauna Loa macadamias, lightly toasted
¹/4 cup lightly packed cilantro leaves
3 scallions, chopped
3 tablespoons sugar
2 tablespoons rice vinegar
1 tablespoon sesame oil
1 teaspoon chopped garlic
1 teaspoon chopped fresh ginger
¹/2 teaspoon sambal oelek
¹/4 cup soy sauce
8 ounces spaghetti, cooked in boiling water until *al dente*, then drained

In the bowl of a food processor, combine macadamias, cilantro, scallions, sugar, rice vinegar, sesame oil, garlic, ginger, and sambal oelek and process until smooth. With motor running, add soy sauce and process until thoroughly combined. Pour mixture into a large serving bowl. Add the hot spaghetti and toss well. Serve immediately.

SERVES 4 TO 6

Macadamia-Crusted Tofu with Noodles

🍃 *This healthful and flavorful summer dish is a study in contrasts. The crunch of the macadamias is a surprising complement to the creaminess of the tofu.*

1 package (about 14 ounces) extra-firm
 tofu, drained
1/4 cup sake
2 tablespoons soy sauce
1 teaspoon sesame oil

Dressing:

2 tablespoons prepared black bean sauce
2 tablespoons sake
2 tablespoons sesame oil
1 tablespoon soy sauce
1 tablespoon sugar

8 ounces dried Chinese egg noodles or
 spaghetti
2 bunches watercress, coarsely chopped
1 bunch scallions, thinly sliced
1/4 cup finely ground Mauna Loa
 macadamias
2 tablespoons Mauna Loa Macadamia Oil

✎ Slice tofu crosswise into 8 pieces. Drain on paper towels. In a shallow dish, stir together sake, soy sauce, and sesame oil. Place tofu in dish, cover and marinate in the refrigerator for 2 hours. Remove tofu from marinade and drain briefly. Reserve excess marinade.

For the dressing: In a large bowl, whisk together all dressing ingredients until smooth. Add reserved marinade.

Cook noodles in boiling water until *al dente*, then drain. Place hot noodles in dressing and toss to coat. Add watercress and scallions and toss.

Place ground macadamias on a plate. Dip tofu into macadamias and press lightly to coat one side. In a large skillet, heat macadamia oil over medium heat. Cook tofu, macadamia-side down, for about 3 minutes or until golden brown. Turn and cook on the other side until golden brown.

To serve, divide noodles between 4 plates and place 2 pieces of tofu, macadamia-side up, on top of each.

SERVES 4

$\int$ ea Bass with Warm Lemon Curry Vinaigrette

≫ *Alejandro Fernandez at the Outrigger Prince Kuhio Hotel in Honolulu, has offset the sweetness of the sea bass with the tangy acidity of the lemon vinaigrette.*

Warm Lemon Curry Vinaigrette:

1/4 cup freshly squeezed lemon juice

1/4 cup heavy cream

3/4 teaspoon curry powder

Salt

1/2 cup extra-virgin olive oil

1 teaspoon white wine vinegar

1/2 cup finely chopped Mauna Loa macadamias, lightly toasted

4 tablespoons extra-virgin olive oil

4 (6-ounce) sea bass filets

Salt and freshly ground pepper

≫ *For the warm lemon curry vinaigrette:*
In a small saucepan, combine lemon juice, cream, curry powder, and salt to taste. Simmer over low heat until hot. Pour into a blender. With motor running, add oil in a thin, steady stream until all is incorporated.

Blend in the vinegar. Return to saucepan and stir in macadamias. Keep warm.

For the fish: In a large skillet, heat 4 tablespoons oil. Place sea bass filets into skillet and cook 4 to 5 minutes per side, or until fish starts to flake. Season with salt and pepper. Divide sea bass onto 4 plates and drizzle with the warm lemon curry vinaigrette. Serve with steamed asparagus.

SERVES 4

> Macadamia oil has no more
> calories than any other fat,
> costs only about as much as
> extra-virgin olive oil,
> and can be used anywhere oil
> is called for.

Sweet and Spicy Glazed Chicken Wings

✎ *This ever-popular Chinese appetizer gets loads of extra crunch from the macadamias.*

Marinade:

1 cup lightly packed cilantro leaves
1/4 cup chopped fresh garlic
1/4 cup chopped fresh ginger
1 teaspoon dried red chile flakes
1 cup soy sauce
1/2 cup rice vinegar

4 pounds chicken wings

Sweet and Spicy Glaze:

2 cups rice vinegar
1 1/2 cups sugar
2 teaspoons dried red chile flakes
1 clove garlic, minced

3/4 cup finely chopped Mauna Loa macadamias

❦ *For the marinade:* In the bowl of a food processor, combine cilantro, garlic, ginger, and chile flakes and process until smooth. With motor running, add soy sauce and vinegar and process until well combined. Pour marinade into a large non-reactive bowl.

Add chicken wings and stir to coat. Cover and marinate in the refrigerator overnight, stirring occasionally.

For the sweet and spicy glaze: In a saucepan, whisk together vinegar, sugar, chile flakes, and garlic. Bring to a boil, then reduce heat to medium and simmer for about 25 minutes, or until mixture is reduced by half.

Preheat oven to 400 degrees F. Lightly oil a broiling pan.

Remove chicken wings from marinade and place on prepared broiling pan. Bake for about 20 minutes, or until done.

Place hot chicken wings into a large bowl. Pour over hot glaze and toss to coat well. Sprinkle macadamias over and toss again. Serve immediately.

SERVES 8

Mussaman Beef Curry

This fragrant curry is from the southern, mostly Muslim, part of Thailand.

1/3 cup hot water
1 tablespoon dried tamarind
3 tablespoons Mauna Loa Macadamia Oil
1 1/2-pounds round steak *or* stewing beef,
   cut into 1-inch cubes
1 tablespoon mussaman curry paste
1 onion, chopped
3 cups unsweetened coconut milk
2 tablespoons fish sauce
1 tablespoon sugar
1/2 teaspoon cardamom
1 large potato, peeled and cut into
   1/2-inch cubes
1/2 cup chopped Mauna Loa macadamias

In a small bowl, combine hot water and tamarind. Let stand 30 minutes then strain. Reserve liquid and discard solids. Set aside.

In a large pot, heat oil over medium-high heat. Add beef and brown well on all sides. Add curry paste and stir to coat beef well. Add onion and stir to mix. Stir in coconut milk, reserved tamarind liquid, fish sauce, sugar, and cardamom and bring to a boil. Reduce heat to low, cover, and simmer 1 to 1 1/2 hours, stirring often, until beef is very tender. Add potato and macadamias, cover, and simmer an additional 30 minutes, stirring often, or until potato is tender.

Serve over steamed rice.

SERVES 6 TO 8

Macadamias have the same total
fat content as pecans,
but contain nearly double
the amount of
monounsaturated fatty acids.
In fact, of all of the most common
nuts, macadamias are highest
in monounsaturated fats and lowest
in saturated fats.

Butternut Squash Gratin

✍ *This lovely side dish can stand on its own as the centerpiece for a delicious vegetarian entrée.*

1 cup heavy cream

2 tablespoons minced fresh sage

1 teaspoon minced fresh thyme

2 cloves garlic, minced

1/2 teaspoon salt

1/2 teaspoon freshly ground pepper

1 small (about 2-pounds) butternut squash; peeled, seeded, thinly sliced, and divided in thirds

6 ounces feta cheese, crumbled and divided in half

6 ounces mozzarella, shredded and divided in thirds

1/2 cup finely chopped Mauna Loa macadamias

◖ Preheat oven to 325 degrees F. Lightly oil a 2 1/2-quart baking dish.

In a bowl, whisk together cream, sage, thyme, garlic, salt, and pepper. Set aside.

Place a layer of squash in the bottom of the prepared baking dish. Layer half of the feta and one-third of the mozzarella. Add another layer of squash, then the remaining feta, and one-third of the mozzarella. Layer remaining third of squash. Pour cream mixture over the top of the squash. Sprinkle macadamias and the remaining mozzarella over the top. Bake for about 45 minutes, or until the top is browned and the squash is tender when pierced with a knife.

SERVES 8

Macadamia-Crusted Rack of Lamb

$^1/_2$ cup finely chopped Mauna Loa
macadamias

$^1/_3$ cup lightly packed fresh Italian parsley
leaves

1 tablespoon Dijon mustard

3 cloves garlic

1 teaspoon salt

$^1/_2$ teaspoon freshly ground pepper

1 rack of lamb with 8 ribs

Preheat oven to 400 degrees F.

Place macadamias, parsley, Dijon, garlic, salt, and pepper in the bowl of a food processor and process until almost smooth. Set aside.

Lightly score the fat side of the rack of lamb. Cover rib tips with foil. Place fat-side up on a broiling pan. Roast for 20 minutes. Remove from oven and pat macadamia mixture on top of the lamb. Return to oven and continue to roast an additional 10 to 15 minutes, or until internal temperature reaches 140 degrees F. Remove from oven and let lamb rest for 10 minutes before carving.

SERVES 4

Macadamias and macadamia nut oil have a 1 to 1 ratio of omega-3 to omega-6 fatty acids. These essential fatty acids are responsible for the shine in our hair as well as our cardiovascular health. Macadamia oil is even healthier than olive oil, which has only a 1 to 5 ratio of omega-3 to omega-6 acids. Since most of us already receive more omega-6 fatty acids than we need, macadamia nuts and macadamia oil are ideal in helping to supply the proper amounts of omega-3 fatty acids.

ᘉ *Sweets*

Sweet Potato and Macadamia Muffins

These chewy muffins combine two favorite Hawaiian flavors.

2/3 cup sugar
1/3 cup butter, softened
1 egg
1 teaspoon vanilla extract
1 3/4 cups all-purpose flour
1 1/2 teaspoons baking powder
1/2 teaspoon salt
2/3 cup milk
1 1/2 cups lightly packed, finely grated
   sweet potato
1/2 cup chopped Mauna Loa
   macadamias

Preheat oven to 375 degrees F. Lightly oil a muffin tin.

In a large bowl, cream sugar and butter together until light and fluffy. Beat in egg and vanilla until smooth. In a bowl, stir flour, baking powder, and salt together with a fork. Add to sugar mixture alternately with milk, beating until just combined. Fold in sweet potato and macadamias.

Pour batter into muffin tins almost filling them. Bake for about 25 minutes, or until a toothpick inserted in the center comes out clean. Serve warm.

MAKES ABOUT 12 MUFFINS

> Although the macadamia nut has become virtually synonymous with Hawaii, Australia is also a major source for this most delectable nut.
>
> Other countries and places where the macadamia is grown include southern California, Costa Rica, Brazil, Guatemala, South Africa, Kenya, Malawi, and Zimbabwe.

Hawaiian Granola

With seasonal fruit for breakfast or on its own as a high-energy snack, this granola will earn rave reviews from family and friends.

5 cups oatmeal
2 cups sweetened flaked coconut
2 cups chopped Mauna Loa macadamias
2 cups dried bananas
3/4 cup butter
1/4 cup honey
1/4 cup packed brown sugar
1 cup chopped dried pineapple

Preheat oven to 350 degrees F. Lightly oil two jelly roll pans.

In a large bowl, combine oatmeal, coconut, and macadamias. Place bananas in the bowl of a food processor and pulse until coarsely chopped. Stir bananas into oatmeal mixture. In a medium saucepan, whisk together the butter, honey, and brown sugar over medium heat until smooth. Pour the butter mixture over the oatmeal mixture and stir until evenly moistened.

Divide the mixture between the prepared pans and bake for 10 minutes. Remove pans from oven and stir well. Return pans to oven and bake an additional 10 minutes, or until golden brown. Let the granola cool then return to large bowl. Stir in the pineapple. Cool completely then store in an airtight container.

MAKES ABOUT 14 CUPS

Banana Macadamia Muffins

These moist, cake-like muffins are favorites at the Kahala Mandarin Oriental Hotel in Honolulu. They will be right at home on your breakfast table, too.

1 cup (2 bananas) mashed bananas
1 1/3 cups cake flour
1 cup sugar
1/2 cup bread flour
1 1/4 teaspoons baking soda
2 eggs
1/4 cup Mauna Loa Macadamia Oil
1/2 cup buttermilk
1 cup finely chopped Mauna Loa macadamias

Preheat oven to 350 degrees F. Lightly oil a muffin tin.

In a large bowl, combine bananas, cake flour, sugar, bread flour, and baking soda and beat until smooth. Add eggs and beat until smooth. Add macadamia oil and beat until smooth. Add buttermilk and beat until smooth. Stir in macadamias.

Pour batter into muffin tins almost filling them. Bake for about 20 minutes, or until a toothpick inserted in the center of a muffin comes out clean.

MAKES ABOUT 18 MUFFINS

The macadamia is a beautiful evergreen tree that grows to a height of about 40 feet. It takes four to seven years for the tree to bear fruit and it will yield a crop for up to 150 years. In fact, Hawaiian trees first planted in the nineteenth century are still alive and bearing!

M acadamia and Currant Scones

Macadamias transform an English tea time classic into a South Pacific specialty.

2 1/2 cups all-purpose flour
4 1/2 teaspoons baking powder
1 teaspoon salt
2/3 cup sugar
1/2 cup cold butter, cut into small pieces
1/2 cup finely chopped Mauna Loa
    macadamias
1/2 cup currants
1/2 cup heavy cream
3 eggs, in all
2 teaspoons milk

❧ Preheat oven to 350 degrees F. Lightly butter two baking sheets.

In a large bowl, sift together the flour, baking powder, and salt. Stir in the sugar. Cut in the butter until the mixture resembles coarse meal. Stir in the macadamias and currants. Make a well in the center. In a separate bowl, blend the cream with 2 eggs until smooth. Pour cream mixture into the well in the flour mixture. Stir until mixture holds together. Gather dough into a ball, it will be moist. Divide in half and flatten into discs.

Turn dough out onto a lightly floured board and roll out to a 1-inch thickness. Cut out rounds using a 3-inch cookie cutter. Transfer to prepared baking sheets. Blend remaining egg and milk together and brush tops of scones with mixture. Bake for about 20 minutes or until golden brown.

MAKES 12 SCONES

Macadamia Bread

Honolulu's Kahala Mandarin Oriental Hotel serves this delicious quick bread as the perfect accompaniment to a cup of Earl Grey tea.

1 cup plus 2 tablespoons sugar
3/4 cup butter, softened
3 eggs
1 1/2 teaspoons vanilla extract
3/4 teaspoon almond extract
2 1/2 cups all-purpose flour
1 teaspoon baking powder
1/4 teaspoon salt
2/3 cup heavy cream
1 1/2 cups chopped Mauna Loa
   macadamias

*Preheat oven to 325 degrees F. Butter and flour two 8 x 4-inch loaf pans.

In a large bowl, cream together sugar and butter. Beat in eggs, vanilla, and almond extract until light and fluffy. Sift flour, baking powder, and salt together into a small bowl. Add flour mixture to butter mixture alternately with cream, beating well after each addition. Stir in macadamias. Divide batter into prepared pans and bake for 35 to 40 minutes, or until toothpick inserted in the center comes out clean. Cool in pans.

MAKES 2 LOAVES

To toast macadamias, preheat your oven to 350 degrees F, place the macadamias on a baking sheet, and toast, shaking the pan occasionally. They should be lightly toasted in about 7 minutes. Since they burn easily, watch them closely!

Juicy Apple Crisp

This old-time favorite becomes a brand new classic with the addition of macadamias. Serve with vanilla ice cream.

1/4 cup sugar
1 tablespoon all-purpose flour
1/2 teaspoon cinnamon
2 pounds Granny Smith apples, peeled, cored and thinly sliced

Topping:

1/4 cup packed brown sugar
5 tablespoons all-purpose flour
1 teaspoon cinnamon
1/4 teaspoon nutmeg
6 tablespoons cold butter
3/4 cup oatmeal
1/2 cup finely chopped Mauna Loa macadamias

◖◖◗ Preheat oven to 350 degrees F.
Generously butter a 9 x 9-inch baking pan.

In a large bowl, combine sugar, flour, and
cinnamon. Stir with a fork until blended.
Add apples and toss to coat. Pour into
prepared pan.

For the topping: In a bowl, stir together
brown sugar, flour, cinnamon, and nutmeg.
Cut in the butter just until crumbly. Stir in the
oatmeal and macadamias. Spread topping
over the apples, making sure that edges are
covered. Bake 40 to 45 minutes, or until
apples are tender.

SERVES 6

C herry and Macadamia Clafoutis

❦ Always best when cherries are at their peak, this country French dessert gets a tropical twist with the addition of macadamias.

4 eggs
1 cup sugar
1/2 cup heavy cream
1/2 cup milk
1 teaspoon vanilla extract
1/4 teaspoon almond extract
1/4 cup all-purpose flour
1/4 cup melted butter
3 cups pitted cherries
1/2 cup chopped Mauna Loa macadamias

❦ Preheat oven to 325 degrees F. Generously butter a 10-inch pie pan.

In a large bowl, beat eggs until frothy. Add sugar and beat until pale in color. Stir in cream, milk, vanilla, and almond extract. Beat in flour until smooth. Beat in butter until smooth.

Pour half of the batter into prepared pie pan. Place cherries evenly over batter. Top with remaining batter. Sprinkle macadamias over the top. Bake for about 1 hour, or until golden brown.

SERVES 10

Delicate in flavor, macadamia oil
allows the flavors of other
ingredients to shine.
With a 389-degree F smoke point,
it is better for a stir-fry or
a quick sauté than olive oil,
which starts to burn at a mere
200 degrees F.
Low in carbohydrates and high
in essential and nutritious
fatty acids, macadamia nuts are
an ideal ingredient.

Nutty Peaches

Elizabeth Thomas, of the Elizabeth Thomas Cooking School in Berkeley, California, offers this lovely way to savor the all-too-short season of tree-ripened peaches.

4 peaches
1/4 cup freshly squeezed orange juice
1/4 cup packed brown sugar
2 tablespoons orange liqueur
1/2 cup heavy cream
1/4 cup sour cream
2 tablespoons sugar
1/2 cup chopped Mauna Loa macadamias

Peel, pit, and slice the peaches. Distribute evenly between 6 pretty glass dishes. In a bowl, whisk together orange juice, brown sugar, and liqueur until sugar dissolves. Pour over the peaches. In a bowl, whip the cream just until stiff. In a small bowl, whisk the sour cream with the sugar, then fold into the whipped cream. Spoon the cream over the peaches and sprinkle with macadamias.

SERVES 6

Macadamia Pie

Mauna Loa Macadamia Recipe Contest winner Dalo Dela Paz transforms a Southern classic into an Island treat.

1 1/4 cups light corn syrup
1 cup packed brown sugar
4 eggs
2 tablespoons melted butter
2 cups chopped Mauna Loa macadamias
1 ten-inch unbaked pie shell
Whipped cream, for topping

Preheat oven to 350 degrees F.

In a large bowl, whisk together corn syrup, brown sugar, and eggs until smooth. Stir in butter and macadamias. Pour into pie shell and bake for 50 to 60 minutes, or until knife inserted in the center comes out clean. Let pie cool completely before cutting. Serve with whipped cream.

SERVES 12

Macadamia Cheesecake

❧ I have converted many a doubting cheesecake purist to this delightful variation.

Crust:

1 1/2 cups (6 ounces) amaretti cookie crumbs
1/2 cup finely chopped Mauna Loa macadamias
1/2 cup packed brown sugar
1/3 cup melted butter

Filling:

1 1/2 pounds cream cheese
3/4 cup sugar
1 tablespoon all-purpose flour
4 eggs
1/3 cup macadamia liqueur
1 teaspoon vanilla extract

◖ Preheat oven to 350 degrees F.

For the crust: Combine the cookie crumbs, macadamias, and brown sugar in the bowl of a food processor. Pulse a few times to mix ingredients. Add the butter and pulse to blend. Press mixture into the bottom of a 10-inch springform pan.

For the filling: In a large bowl, beat the cream cheese, sugar, and flour together until smooth, scraping the sides often. Add the eggs, one at a time, beating well after each addition. Add the macadamia liqueur and vanilla and beat until smooth.

Pour the batter into the prepared crust and place springform pan on a baking sheet. Bake for about 1 hour, or until cheesecake is very lightly golden and begins to pull away from the sides of the pan. Cool to room temperature, then cover and chill overnight.

SERVES 12

Pumpkin Cheesecake with Macadamia Gingersnap Crust

This is a deliciously happy marriage between two dessert classics.

Crust:

1 1/2 cups (6 ounces) gingersnap crumbs

1/2 cup finely chopped Mauna Loa macadamias

1/4 cup packed brown sugar

1/3 cup melted butter

Filling:

1 pound cream cheese

8 ounces mascarpone cheese

1 cup sugar

1 cup pumpkin

3 eggs

2 teaspoons cinnamon

1 teaspoon ground ginger

🍳 Preheat oven to 350 degrees F.

For the crust: Place the gingersnap crumbs, macadamias, and brown sugar in the bowl of a food processor. Pulse a few times to mix ingredients. Add the melted butter and pulse to blend. Press the mixture into the bottom of a 10-inch springform pan.

For the filling: In a large bowl, beat the cream cheese, mascarpone, and sugar together until smooth, scraping the sides often. Add pumpkin and beat until smooth. Add the eggs, one at a time, beating well after each addition. Add the cinnamon and ginger and beat until smooth.

Pour batter into the prepared crust and place springform pan on a baking sheet. Bake for 45 to 50 minutes, or until cheesecake is very lightly golden and begins to pull away from the sides of the pan. Cool to room temperature, then cover and chill overnight.

SERVES 12

Espresso Cheesecake

⟞ This is destined to become every coffee lover's ultimate cheesecake recipe.

Crust:

1 1/2 cups (6 ounces) chocolate cookie
   crumbs

1/4 cup sugar

1/3 cup melted butter

Filling:

1 1/2 pounds cream cheese

1 1/4 cups sugar

2 tablespoons all-purpose flour

3 eggs

3/4 cup heavy cream

1/4 cup brewed espresso

1/2 teaspoon freshly squeezed lemon
   juice

1/2 teaspoon vanilla extract

1/2 cup finely chopped Mauna Loa
   macadamias

Preheat oven to 350 degrees F.

For the crust: Place the cookie crumbs and sugar in the bowl of a food processor. Pulse a few times to mix ingredients. Add the melted butter and pulse to blend. Press the mixture into the bottom of a 10-inch springform pan.

For the filling: In a large bowl, beat the cream cheese, sugar, and flour together until smooth, scraping the sides often. Add the eggs one at a time, beating well after each addition. Beat in the cream, espresso, lemon juice, and vanilla until smooth. Pour batter into the prepared crust and place springform pan on a baking sheet. Bake for about 45 minutes, or until cheesecake is very lightly golden and begins to pull away from the sides of the pan. Cool to room temperature, then cover and chill overnight.

Remove the cheesecake from the refrigerator. Carefully remove the band of the springform pan and place cheesecake on a baking sheet. Press macadamias into the side of the cheesecake. Carefully slide a long spatula under the crust of the cheesecake and slide onto a serving platter.

Serves 12

Lime Cheesecake with Macadamia Gingersnap Crust

☜ Somehow this cheesecake manages to be both rich and refreshing at the same time. I serve it after a spicy Asian meal.

Crust:

1 1/2 cups (6 ounces) gingersnap crumbs

1/2 cup finely chopped Mauna Loa macadamias

1/4 cup packed brown sugar

1/3 cup melted butter

Filling:

1 1/2 pounds cream cheese

1 cup sugar

4 eggs

6 tablespoons freshly squeezed lime juice

2 teaspoons finely minced lime zest

✒ Preheat oven to 350 degrees F.

For the crust: Place the gingersnap crumbs, macadamias, and brown sugar in the bowl of a food processor. Pulse a few times to mix ingredients. Add the melted butter and pulse to blend. Press the mixture into the bottom of a 10-inch springform pan.

For the filling: In a large bowl, beat the cream cheese and sugar together until smooth, scraping the sides often. Add the eggs, one at a time, beating well after each addition. Add the lime juice and zest and beat until smooth.

Pour batter into the prepared crust and place springform pan on a baking sheet. Bake for about 45 minutes, or until cheesecake is very lightly golden and begins to pull away from the sides of the pan. Cool to room temperature, then cover and chill overnight.

SERVES 12

Paradise Cake

This exotic variation on the traditional fruitcake is laden with tropical fruit and macadamias.

6 eggs
1 cup sugar
1/4 cup honey
3 tablespoons Mauna Loa Macadamia Oil
1 tablespoon vanilla extract
1 1/3 cups all-purpose flour
2 1/2 teaspoons baking powder
1 teaspoon salt
2 cups sweetened shredded coconut
10 ounces dried pineapple, finely diced
1 cup finely chopped Mauna Loa macadamias

✆ Preheat oven to 300 degrees F. Line the bottom of an angel food cake pan with a removable bottom with parchment paper, then oil the bottom and sides of pan.

In a large bowl, beat eggs and sugar together until frothy. Beat in honey, oil, and vanilla until smooth. Add flour, baking powder, and salt and beat until smooth. Stir in coconut, pineapple, and macadamias until well combined.

Pour batter into prepared pan and bake for about 1 hour and 10 minutes or until a toothpick inserted in the center comes out clean. Cool in the pan, then run a knife around the edge of the pan and around the center hole to loosen the cake. Invert onto a serving plate and peel off parchment.

SERVES 12

Iced Lemon Macadamia Pound Cake

This is a dazzling little cake to serve in thin wedges with tea. The intense lemon flavor is mellowed with creamy flavor of the macadamias.

Pound Cake:

1 cup chopped Mauna Loa macadamias

1 cup sugar

1 cup butter, softened

4 eggs

$1/4$ cup freshly squeezed lemon juice

1 tablespoon finely minced lemon zest

1 cup all-purpose flour

1 teaspoon baking powder

$1/4$ teaspoon salt

Icing:

$1\,1/2$ cups powdered sugar

3 tablespoons freshly squeezed lemon juice

Preheat the oven to 350 degrees F. Butter and flour a 9-inch round cake pan.

For the pound cake: In the bowl of a food processor, combine the macadamias and sugar and process until finely ground. In a large bowl, cream the butter and macadamia mixture until light and fluffy, scraping the sides of the bowl often. Add the eggs, one at a time, beating well after each addition. Beat in the lemon juice and zest. Sift the flour, baking powder, and salt over the batter and beat until smooth.

Pour batter into the prepared pan and bake for 40 to 45 minutes, or until a toothpick inserted in the center comes out clean. Cool for 15 minutes in the pan, then run a knife around the edges and invert onto a rack. Cool completely.

For the icing: Whisk the powdered sugar and lemon juice together until completely smooth.

Place the rack on a baking sheet. Brush off any crumbs. With a small spatula, spread icing over the top and sides of the cake. Wait about 15 minutes and ice the sides again. Pour remaining icing over the top evenly. Let cake stand about 1 hour to allow the icing to harden.

SERVES 8

Black-Bottom Coconut Cream Tart with Macadamia Crust

  This is a sophisticated but easy confection with a rich and buttery macadamia crust with a chocolate layer and and old-fashioned coconut cream filling.

Macadamia Crust:

1 1/2 cups all-purpose flour
1/2 cup cold butter, cut into small pieces
1/4 cup sugar
1 egg
1 teaspoon vanilla extract
1/8 teaspoon salt
1 cup finely ground Mauna Loa
  macadamias

Chocolate Layer:

2 1/2 ounces bittersweet chocolate, chopped
1/4 cup heavy cream

Coconut Cream Filling:

2 tablespoons cornstarch
1/3 cup sugar
1 cup milk, scalded
2 egg yolks, lightly beaten

1 tablespoon butter

1/4 teaspoon vanilla extract

1/2 cup packed sweetened shredded coconut

1/4 cup packed sweetened shredded coconut, lightly toasted

For the crust: In a large bowl, combine flour, butter, sugar, egg, vanilla, and salt. Beat until mixture is well combined and crumbly. Stir in macadamias.

Press mixture firmly into the bottom and up the sides of a 9-inch tart pan with a removable bottom. Chill for 1 hour.

Preheat oven to 400 degrees F.

Bake tart crust in the middle of the oven for 20 to 25 minutes, or until golden brown. Remove from oven and cool.

For the chocolate layer: Put chopped chocolate in a small bowl. In a small saucepan, bring cream to a boil. Immediately pour over chocolate and whisk until smooth. Spread chocolate over the bottom of the crust.

(continued)

For the filling: In a small saucepan, whisk together cornstarch and sugar. Whisk in milk and cook over medium-high heat, whisking constantly, until slightly thickened. Pour about one quarter of the milk mixture into the egg yolks and whisk until blended. Pour egg yolk mixture back into the saucepan. Reduce heat to medium-low, and cook, whisking constantly, until thick. Remove from heat and whisk in butter and vanilla. Stir in coconut. Pour into tart, spreading the filling to the edges. Sprinkle with toasted coconut. Chill completely before serving.

SERVES 10

Macadamia Butter Nuts

These delightful teacakes are easy for children to make and are a must on a holiday cookie platter.

1 cup butter, softened
1 cup powdered sugar, sifted
1 teaspoon vanilla extract
2 1/2 cups all-purpose flour
1/4 teaspoon salt
1 cup finely chopped Mauna Loa
   macadamias
Powdered sugar

Preheat oven to 400 degrees F.

In a large bowl, cream together butter and sugar. Beat in vanilla. Beat in flour and salt until smooth. Stir in macadamias. Shape dough into 1 1/2-inch balls. Place on baking sheets and bake for about 9 minutes, or until just beginning to color. Remove from oven and, while still warm, roll in powdered sugar. Place on waxed paper to cool. Store in an airtight container.

MAKES ABOUT 48 COOKIES

M acadamia and Raspberry Tart

🌀 *This is one of my favorite breakfast pastries, either on its own, or as an admittedly decadent accompaniment to eggs Benedict.*

Sweet Pastry Dough:

1 1/3 cups all-purpose flour

3 tablespoons sugar

1/4 teaspoon salt

1/2 cup cold butter, cut into small pieces

1 large egg

2 tablespoons cold water

1 teaspoon vanilla extract

Filling:

1 cup finely chopped Mauna Loa macadamias

1/2 cup sugar

4 eggs

1/2 cup all-purpose flour

3/4 cup raspberry jam

1/2 cup chopped Mauna Loa macadamias

۵۵ Preheat oven to 350 degrees F.

For the sweet pastry dough: In a large bowl, stir together flour, sugar, and salt. Cut in the butter until mixture resembles coarse meal. In a small bowl, whisk together the egg, water, and vanilla. Stir into flour mixture until dough holds together. Gather dough into a ball, wrap it in plastic wrap, form into a disc, and chill for about 30 minutes.

Turn dough out onto a lightly floured surface and roll out to fit a 10-inch tart pan with a removable bottom.

For the filling: In the bowl of a food processor, combine the 1 cup of macadamias and sugar, and process until finely ground. Pour mixture into a large bowl. Add eggs, one at a time, beating well after each addition. Add flour and beat until smooth.

Spread raspberry jam over the bottom of the crust. Spread the macadamia mixture evenly over the jam. Sprinkle the 1/2 cup macadamias on top. Bake for 35 to 40 minutes, or until golden. Cool completely before removing tart from the pan.

SERVES 12

Triple-Chocolate
Macadamia Icebox Cookies

These are the ultimate in drop-dead decadent chocolate cookies. Make these in advance to satisfy the chocolate urge whenever it strikes.

1 cup semisweet chocolate chips

2 ounces unsweetened chocolate

2 tablespoons butter

3/4 cup sugar

2 eggs

1 teaspoon vanilla extract

1/3 cup all-purpose flour

1/4 teaspoon baking powder

1/8 teaspoon salt

2 cups finely chopped Mauna Loa macadamias

1/2 cup white chocolate chips

In the top of a double boiler, melt together semisweet chocolate chips, unsweetened chocolate, and butter over simmering water. Stir to blend well. Set aside to cool.

In a large bowl, beat together the sugar, eggs, and vanilla until mixture is pale and thick. Beat in cooled chocolate mixture until smooth. Add flour, baking powder, and salt. Beat until well blended. Stir in macadamias and white chocolate chips. The dough will be very soft and sticky. With a rubber spatula, spread dough into a log about 15 inches long onto a piece of plastic wrap. Roll up tightly, then securely wrap in another piece of plastic wrap. Freeze at least 3 hours and up to 2 months.

Preheat oven to 350 degrees F. Lightly oil two baking sheets.

Remove dough from freezer. Slice dough 3/4-inch thick and place on prepared baking sheets. Bake for about 12 minutes, or until cookies are set. Cool on baking sheets.

MAKES ABOUT 24 COOKIES

Macadamia Biscotti

Fred Halpert at the Brava Terrace in St. Helena, California, twice-baked these biscotti for extra crunch.

1/2 cup butter, softened

1 cup packed brown sugar

1/3 cup sugar

1 teaspoon vanilla extract

3/4 teaspoon finely minced orange zest

1 egg

1 1/2 cups all-purpose flour

2/3 cup ground almonds

1 teaspoon baking powder

1/2 teaspoon cinnamon

1/4 teaspoon salt

1 cup finely chopped Mauna Loa macadamias

In a large bowl, cream together butter, brown sugar, sugar, vanilla, and orange zest. Add egg and beat until smooth. Add flour, ground almonds, baking powder, cinnamon, and salt and blend until smooth. Stir in macadamias.

Divide the dough in half and roll into 12-inch cylinders. Cover with plastic and refrigerate for at least 3 hours.

Preheat oven to 325 degrees F. Line two baking sheets with parchment paper.

Remove dough and discard plastic wrap. Place dough at least 3 inches apart on prepared baking sheets. Bake for 35 minutes or until golden and dry to the touch. Remove from oven and allow to cool slightly.

Cut the logs diagonally into 3/4-inch slices. Arrange the biscotti, cut side up, on the baking sheets so that they do not touch each other. Place back in oven and bake an additional 25 minutes, or until crisp and dry. Cool on racks.

MAKES 2 DOZEN BISCOTTI

Macadamia Coconut Icebox Cookies

🌿 *In addition to the great flavor marriage of macadamias and coconut, these cookies are ideal to keep as dough in the freezer and need only a few minutes to bake — thanks to Bev Kype at Merriman's Restaurant on the Big Island.*

1 1/2 cups butter, softened

1 1/4 cups sugar

1 tablespoon vanilla extract

2 cups all-purpose flour

1 teaspoon baking soda

1/4 teaspoon salt

2 cups oatmeal

2 cups chopped Mauna Loa macadamias

1 cup sweetened flaked coconut

In a large bowl, cream butter and sugar together until fluffy. Beat in vanilla. Sift together flour, baking soda, and salt and add to butter mixture. Beat until smooth. Add oatmeal, macadamias, and coconut and beat until well blended. Divide dough into 3 portions. Place each portion on a piece of plastic wrap and form into a log about 10 inches long. Wrap and freeze for at least 2 hours, and up to 2 months.

Preheat oven to 325 degrees F. Line baking sheets with parchment paper.

Remove frozen dough and let stand at room temperature for 5 minutes. Slice each log crosswise into 24 rounds. Place on prepared baking sheets about 1 inch apart. Bake for 12 to 15 minutes or until golden brown.

MAKES 72 COOKIES

White Chip Macadamia Bars

Knowing my passion for white chocolate, the Ghirardelli Chocolate Company gave me this dreamy bar cookie recipe.

1 1/2 cups packed brown sugar
1 cup butter, softened
2 eggs
2 teaspoons vanilla extract
3 cups all-purpose flour
1 1/2 teaspoons baking powder
1 teaspoon salt
2 cups Ghirardelli Classic White Chips
1 cup chopped Mauna Loa macadamias

Preheat oven to 350 degrees F.

In a large bowl, cream brown sugar and butter together until light and fluffy. Add eggs, one at a time, beating well after each addition. Stir in vanilla. Stir in flour, baking powder, and salt until well blended. Fold in white chips and macadamias. Spread batter evenly into a 13 x 9-inch baking pan. Bake for 25 to 30 minutes. Remove from oven and let cool at least 40 minutes before cutting into squares.

MAKES 36 BARS

Macadamia Toffee

🌀 *A layer of chocolate, dusted with macadamias covers this crunchy toffee and makes a pretty holiday gift, ready for wrapping.*

1 cup butter
1 cup sugar
2 tablespoons water
1 tablespoon light corn syrup
1/2 cup chopped Mauna Loa macadamias
1/3 cup semisweet chocolate chips
1/2 cup finely chopped Mauna Loa macadamias

🌀 Lightly oil a baking sheet.

In a heavy saucepan, combine butter, sugar, water, and corn syrup. Cook over high heat, stirring constantly, until candy thermometer reaches 280 degrees F. Remove from heat and stir in chopped macadamias.

Pour onto prepared baking sheet and spread thinly and evenly. Let cool about 10 minutes then sprinkle chocolate chips over the top. When the chocolate has softened, spread evenly over toffee and sprinkle with the finely chopped macadamias. When completely cool, break into pieces.

MAKES ABOUT 1 1/2 POUNDS OF TOFFEE

Macadamia Rum Bars

Macadamias join forces with sweet coconut and spicy rum to conjure up the heady romance of the tropics.

Crust:

1/2 cup butter, softened

1/4 cup sugar

1 cup all-purpose flour

Filling:

1 1/4 cups packed brown sugar

2 eggs

2 tablespoons all-purpose flour

1 tablespoon dark rum

1 teaspoon vanilla extract

1/2 teaspoon salt

1/4 teaspoon baking powder

1 cup sweetened flaked coconut

1 cup finely chopped Mauna Loa macadamias

Icing:

1 1/4 cups powdered sugar, sifted

2 tablespoons butter, softened

1 tablespoon milk

1 teaspoon dark rum
$1/2$ teaspoon vanilla extract

❧ Preheat oven to 350 degrees F. Lightly oil a 13 x 9-inch baking pan.

For the crust: In a large bowl, cream butter and sugar together until fluffy. Beat in the flour until well blended. Press dough into the bottom of prepared pan. Bake for 15 to 20 minutes or until lightly browned.

For the filling: In a large bowl, beat the brown sugar and eggs together. Beat in the flour, rum, vanilla, salt, and baking powder until smooth. Beat in coconut and macadamias. Spread mixture evenly over crust. Bake an additional 20 minutes, or until golden brown. Remove from oven and cool completely.

For the icing: In a bowl, whisk together powdered sugar, butter, milk, rum, and vanilla until smooth. Spread icing over cooled filling. Cut into 2-inch squares.

MAKES ABOUT 36 BARS

Millionaire's Shortbread

🍥 *Not just for the rich and famous, Mauna Loa Macadamia Recipe Contest winner Kay Cabrera insists that you don't have to be a millionaire, just feel like one while you enjoy her incomparable cookies.*

Shortbread:

2 cups all-purpose flour

$1/2$ cup powdered sugar

$1/4$ teaspoon baking powder

1 cup cold butter, cut into small pieces

$1/2$ teaspoon vanilla extract

Filling:

$2 1/2$ cups sugar

$1/2$ cup water

$3/4$ cup heavy cream

$3/4$ cup plus 2 tablespoons butter,
cut into pieces

2 cups chopped Mauna Loa macadamias,
toasted

Glaze:

8 ounces bittersweet chocolate, chopped

3/4 cup heavy cream

6 tablespoons butter

1/4 cup light corn syrup

🍓 Preheat oven to 350 degrees F. Lightly oil a 13 x 9-inch baking pan.

For the shortbread: In a medium bowl, sift together flour, powdered sugar, and baking powder. Cut in the butter and vanilla until mixture holds together. Press dough evenly into the bottom of the prepared pan. Bake for about 20 minutes, or until the edges are lightly browned and shortbread appears dry and crisp. Remove from oven and cool.

For the filling: In a heavy saucepan, stir together the sugar and water. Bring to a boil over high heat until the sugar begins to caramelize. Swirl the pan gently to allow the syrup to caramelize evenly. When caramel is deep brown, add the cream all at once; stand back since it will sputter and boil up. Remove from heat and swirl pan until the boiling subsides

(continued)

and mixture is evenly blended. Put butter on top of the caramel, letting it melt. Stir until well blended, then stir in the macadamias. Spread filling evenly over shortbread crust. Bake an additional 15 to 20 minutes, or until caramel begins to bubble in the center. Remove from oven and cool completely.

For the glaze: Place the chopped chocolate in a bowl. In a small saucepan, combine the cream, butter, and corn syrup and bring to a boil over medium-high heat. Pour cream mixture over chocolate and whisk gently until smooth. Pour glaze onto caramel and tip pan to spread evenly. Cool completely. To serve, cut into 2-inch squares.

MAKES ABOUT 36 COOKIES

Chocolate Macadamia Fudge

❧ *The secret to making a creamy fudge is the final vigorous beating which prevents sugar crystals from forming.*

2 cups sugar
1 cup evaporated milk
2 tablespoons corn syrup
1/2 teaspoon salt
2 ounces unsweetened chocolate
2 tablespoons butter
1 teaspoon vanilla extract
1 cup chopped Mauna Loa macadamias

❧ Lightly oil an 8-inch square pan.

In a heavy saucepan, stir together sugar, evaporated milk, corn syrup, and salt. Add chocolate and simmer over medium heat, stirring often, until chocolate melts. Raise heat to high and cook, stirring often, until candy thermometer reaches 238 degrees F. Remove from heat and stir in butter. Let mixture cool to lukewarm. Add vanilla and beat vigorously until mixture loses its gloss. Stir in macadamias and spread into prepared pan. Cut into squares when cool.

MAKES ABOUT 1 1/4 POUNDS OF FUDGE

Macadamia and Coffee Chocolate Bars

🍩 *A recipe will only be as good as the ingredients you make it with, so always use the best you can afford. I think Ghirardelli Chocolate is the best in the business.*

1 cup butter, softened

1 cup sugar

1 egg

1/4 cup coffee-flavored liqueur

1 3/4 cups all-purpose flour

6 ounces Ghirardelli Bittersweet Chocolate, broken into 1-inch pieces

3/4 cup finely chopped Mauna Loa macadamias

🍩 Preheat oven to 350 degrees F. Grease a 15 x 10-inch jelly roll pan.

In a large bowl, cream the butter and sugar together until fluffy. Add the egg and liqueur, and mix well. Gradually mix in the flour. Press the dough evenly into prepared pan. Bake 25 minutes, or until golden brown. Immediately top with chocolate and allow to melt. Spread melted chocolate evenly. Sprinkle with macadamias. Place pan on a wire

rack and let cool to room temperature.
Chill 10 minutes, or until chocolate has set.
Store loosely covered.

MAKES ABOUT 32 BARS

Traditionally, macadamia nuts
are gathered by hand after falling
naturally from the tree, although
some growers now use mechanical
sweepers and collectors.
The cost of harvesting the nuts is
exceedingly high since the pickers
must return many times to the
orchards to gather the fresh fallen
nuts. Additionally, since the nuts
don't ripen all at once, the harvest
stretches for seven months.

Macadamia Cheesecake Brownies

This is the most decadent of all the brownie recipes I have tried.

Brownie:

8 ounces semisweet chocolate

6 tablespoons butter

4 eggs

1 1/2 cups sugar

1 cup all-purpose flour

1 teaspoon baking powder

1/2 teaspoon salt

1 1/2 cups finely chopped Mauna Loa
  macadamias

Powdered sugar, for garnish

Cheese Topping:

8 ounces cream cheese

1/2 cup sugar

1/4 cup butter, softened

1 egg

1/2 teaspoon vanilla extract

Powdered sugar, for garnish

Preheat oven to 350 degrees F. Lightly oil a 9-inch springform pan.

For the brownies: In the top of a double boiler, melt together chocolate and butter over simmering water. Remove from heat and let cool. In a large bowl, beat the eggs until foamy. Gradually beat in the sugar until light and fluffy. Stir in the chocolate mixture until blended. Stir in the flour, baking powder, and salt until smooth. Stir in macadamias. Spread batter evenly into prepared pan.

For the cheese topping: In a large bowl, beat cream cheese and sugar together until smooth, scraping the sides often. Beat in butter until fluffy. Gradually beat in egg and vanilla.

Spoon cheese topping over chocolate batter. Swirl together lightly to marble. Bake for 60 to 75 minutes, or until center is just set. Cool on a rack, then cover and chill. Sprinkle with powdered sugar.

SERVES 12

Mauna Loa Macadamia Brittle

🍃 *This is the original Mauna Loa Macadamia Brittle recipe and is one of their most popular products.*

1 1/2 cups sugar

1/2 cup packed brown sugar

2/3 cup light corn syrup

1/4 cup water

1/4 cup butter

1/2 teaspoon salt

1 cup chopped Mauna Loa macadamias

1 teaspoon baking soda

1/2 teaspoon vanilla extract

🍃 Lightly oil a baking sheet.

In a heavy saucepan, combine sugar, brown sugar, corn syrup, and water. Cook over medium-high heat, stirring constantly, until a candy thermometer placed in the syrup near the center of the pan reads 260 degrees F. Add butter and salt and continue to cook until the temperature reaches 295 degrees F. Remove from heat and stir in the macadamias, baking soda, and vanilla.

Pour the brittle onto prepared baking sheet and spread to a $1/4$-inch thickness using a rubber spatula. Cool completely at room temperature. Break into pieces and store in an air-tight container.

MAKES ABOUT 1$1/4$ POUNDS OF BRITTLE

The macadamia tree was first discovered in Australia in 1843 by the Prussian botanical explorer, Friedrich Wilhelm Ludwig Leichardt. The nut was later named for the renowned chemist and Australian parliamentarian Dr. John Macadam.

Hawaii Prince Macadamia Chocolate Pie

Chef Andre Fusero at the Hawaii Prince Hotel Waikiki graciously shared the secrets to his sinfully rich, world-class pie.

1 9-inch prebaked pie shell

Caramel Layer:

1/2 cup sugar

2 tablespoons water

1 tablespoon corn syrup

3 tablespoons heavy cream

2 tablespoons butter

1 1/4 cups chopped Mauna Loa macadamias, lightly toasted

Chocolate Filling:

7 tablespoons sour cream

1 egg

1 egg yolk

2 tablespoons heavy cream

2 tablespoons sugar

2 ounces bittersweet chocolate, chopped

Topping:

1 1/2 cups heavy cream

2 tablespoons sugar

Chocolate shavings, for garnish

For the caramel layer: In a heavy saucepan, whisk together sugar, water, and corn syrup. Bring to a boil over high heat until the sugar begins to caramelize. Swirl the pan gently to allow the syrup to caramelize evenly. When caramel is deep brown, remove from heat. Stir in the cream and butter until smooth. Stir in the macadamias. Pour into pie shell and chill.

For the chocolate filling: In the top of a double boiler, whisk together sour cream, egg, egg yolk, heavy cream, and sugar. Cook over simmering water, stirring constantly, until mixture becomes thick enough to coat the back of a spoon. Remove from heat and whisk in chocolate until smooth. Pour on top of the caramel layer. Chill.

For the topping: In a large bowl, whip cream until soft peaks form. Beat in sugar. Spread over pie and sprinkle with chocolate shavings. Serve immediately.

SERVES 8

Melt-in-Your-Mouth Macadamia Shortbread Cookies

✒ *Daphne Higa at the Grand Wailea Resort on Maui aptly named her deceptively light, notoriously rich shortbread cookies.*

2 cups butter, softened
1 cup plus 2 tablespoons sugar
1 teaspoon vanilla extract
1/2 teaspoon salt
3 cups plus 3 tablespoons all-purpose flour
1 cup cake flour
1 3/4 cups finely chopped Mauna Loa macadamias
1/4 cup raw sugar

✒ Preheat oven to 350 degrees F. Lightly oil two baking sheets.

In a large bowl, cream butter, sugar, vanilla, and salt together until light and fluffy. Add flour and cake flour and beat until smooth. In a shallow dish, stir together macadamias and raw sugar. Form dough into 1-inch balls and roll in macadamia mixture. Place 2-inches apart on prepared baking sheets, and flatten slightly. Bake for about 15 minutes, or until golden brown. Cool on rack.

Makes about 56 cookies

If all you have are the salted macadamias, here's a tip for removing the salt: Place the salted macadamias in a large strainer, rinse for about 10 seconds with warm water, then drain. Transfer the nuts to a baking sheet and dry them at 250 degrees F, shaking the baking sheet occasionally. Transfer to a plate and let them cool completely.

Torta di Santa Maria

🌀 *This luscious cake, dense with chocolate and orange, is a flagship dessert at the Genoa Restaurant in Portland, Oregon. Creator Catherine Whims was kind enough to share it with us.*

Torta:

3/4 cup raisins

1/2 cup orange liqueur

4 1/2 ounces semi-sweet chocolate

2/3 cup sugar

1/2 cup butter, softened

3 eggs

1 cup chopped Mauna Loa macadamias, lightly toasted and finely ground

1/4 cup dry bread crumbs

Zest from 1 orange, finely minced

Glaze:

4 ounces semi-sweet chocolate

1 ounce unsweetened chocolate

2 tablespoons brewed espresso

1/4 cup butter, softened

꧁ Soak the raisins in the orange liqueur overnight.

Preheat the oven to 375 degrees F. Butter an 8-inch round cake pan, line the bottom with parchment paper, and butter the parchment.

For the torta: In the top of a double boiler, melt the chocolate over simmering water. Remove from heat and let cool. In a large bowl, cream the sugar and butter together until fluffy. Add eggs, one at a time, beating well after each addition. Add the raisins and their liqueur, melted chocolate, macadamias, bread crumbs, and orange zest and beat until well blended. Pour batter into prepared cake pan and bake for 30 to 35 minutes, or until edges start pulling away from the pan. The center should look slightly underdone. Cool 15 minutes in the pan, then run a knife around the edges and invert onto a rack. Let cool completely.

For the glaze: In the top of a double-boiler, combine the semi-sweet chocolate, unsweetened chocolate, and espresso. Melt slowly over simmering water and whisk until smooth. Remove from heat and whisk in the butter.

(continued)

Place the rack on a baking sheet. Brush off any crumbs. With a small spatula, spread the glaze over the top and sides of the cake. Pour remaining glaze over the top evenly. Let cake stand for about 1 hour to allow the glaze to set.

SERVES 10

> Out of the way, olive oil!
> Macadamia oil is more
> monounsaturated than
> olive oil.
> Macadamia oil is 80 percent
> monounsaturated, while
> olive oil is only 74 percent.
> Another of our favorites,
> canola oil is a mere
> 58 percent monounsaturated!

◖ *Contributors*

Kahala Mandarin Oriental
   Hotel
5000 Kahala Avenue
Honolulu, HI 96815

Alejandro Fernandez
Outrigger Prince Kuhio
   Hotel
2500 Kuhio Avenue
Honolulu, HI 96815

Fred Halpert
Brava Terrace
3010 St. Helena Hwy. North
St. Helena, CA 94574

Elizabeth Thomas
Elizabeth Thomas Cooking
   School
1372 Summit Road
Berkeley, CA 94708

Merrimanís Restaurant
Box 2349
Kamuela, HI 96743

Andre Fusero
Hawaii Prince Hotel
100 Holomoana Street
Honolulu, HI 96815

Daphne Higa
Grand Wailea Resort
3850 Wailea Alanui
Wailea, Maui, HI 96753

Catherine Whims
Genoa Restaurant
2832 S. E. Belmont Street
Portland, OR 97214

Conversions

Liquid

1 tablespoon = 15 milliliters
1/2 cup = 4 fluid ounces = 125 milliliters
1 cup = 8 fluid ounces = 250 milliliters

Dry

1/4 cup = 4 tablespoons = 2 ounces = 60 grams
1 cup = 1/2 pound = 8 ounces = 250 grams

Flour

1/2 cup = 60 grams
1 cup = 4 ounces = 125 grams

Temperature

400 degrees F = 200 degrees C = gas mark 6
375 degrees F = 190 degrees C = gas mark 5
350 degrees F = 175 degrees C = gas mark 4

Miscellaneous

2 tablespoons butter = 1 ounce = 30 grams
1 inch = 2.5 centimeters
all purpose flour = plain flour
baking soda = bicarbonate of soda
brown sugar = demerara sugar
confectioners' sugar = icing sugar
heavy cream = double cream
molasses = black treacle
raisins = sultanas
rolled oats = oat flakes
semisweet chocolate = plain chocolate
sugar = caster sugar

Macadamia Cookbook